Continuum
The Tower Building, 11 York Road, London SE1 7NX
15 East 26ᵗʰ Street, New York, NY 10010
www.continuumbooks.com

© Sister Mary Bernard Potter SP and Nigel Bavidge 19̶̶̶-

Excerpts from the Rite of Baptism are taken from *Rite of Baptism for Children*. © 1969, amended 1984. International Commission on English in the Liturgy, Inc. (ICEL).

First published 1994 by Geoffrey Chapman
Reprinted 1997, 1999 by Geoffrey Chapman
Reprinted 2001, 2002, 2005 by Continuum

Nihil obstat: Father Anton Cowan, Censor
Imprimatur: Monsignor Ralph Brown, V.G.
        Westminster, 14 December 1993

The *Nihil obstat* and *Imprimatur* are a declaration that a book or pamphlet is considered to be free from doctrinal or moral error. It is not implied that those who have granted the *Nihil obstat* and *Imprimatur* agree with the contents, opinions or statements expressed.

British Library Cataloguing-in-Publication Data
A catalogue record for this book is available from the British Library

ISBN 0 86012402 9
        0-225-66749-5 (pack of 10)

This course is intended to be used with the Leader's Guide (ISBN 0-225-66745-2)

Illustrations by Brandy Pearson
Cover photograph by Derek Jones

Printed and bound in Great Britain by
Martins the Printers, Berwick upon Tweed

CONGRATULATIONS

on the birth of your baby and welcome to this preparation for your baby's Baptism.

Bringing new life into the world is one of the greatest miracles of life. It brings with it so many joys and blessings. It also brings a lot of hard work and many responsibilities. In a real way the work is only just beginning. Over the years you will have to care for this wonderful new life and help your baby to grow and become a loving and happy person, able to find joy and to bring joy to the world.

The love you have for your baby is part of the love that God has. Just as you want your baby to find love, happiness and peace, so does God. In fact, this is precisely why God gave this new life into your care.

In the Sacrament of Baptism, God shows this love. Through this sacrament, your child will become, in a very special way, God's own child and part of the family of the Church. This preparation, which the parish family is offering to you, has been written to help you to think about the important step you are taking in having your baby baptized. It is also meant to help you to reflect on the wonderful love that God wants to share with you and with your baby. We hope you will enjoy the ideas and the sharing and, above all, we hope that you will know more deeply how much God loves you and your baby.

Welcome!

1

OUR BABY

Our baby's name: _____

Date and time of birth: _____

Place of birth: _____

Weight at birth: _____

Length at birth: _____

Before I formed you in the womb
I knew you through and through

HOPES FOR YOUR CHILD

Which of the hopes below do you think are very important?
Put V in the box ☐
Which of the hopes do you think are important?
Put I in the box ☐
Which of the hopes do you think are not so important?
Put N in the box ☐

DO WELL AT SCHOOL	☐	HAVE A GOOD JOB	☐
HAVE LOTS OF FRIENDS	☐	BE GOOD LOOKING	☐
KNOW HOW TO ENJOY LIFE	☐	BE HAPPY	☐
KNOW RIGHT FROM WRONG	☐	MAKE MONEY	☐
HAVE A NICE HOME	☐	BE TRUTHFUL	☐
HAVE A SENSE OF HUMOUR	☐	BE CONFIDENT	☐

If you have any other hopes, write them in the spaces below.

_____

_____

_____

_____

_____

REFLECTION

For it was you who created my being,
knit me together in my mother's womb.
I thank you for the wonder of my being,
for the wonders of all your creation.

Psalm 138(139)

I have been chosen by God to be a parent.

God has entrusted me with a precious gift — a new life.

God will give me every gift I will need to help my child to find true happiness, joy and peace.

What gifts do you want God to give you?

_____

_____

_____

_____

SOMETHING TO DO

You may like to write a letter to your child about your dreams and hopes. Keep it safely; you may want to share it with your child some day.

WELCOME!

'Welcome!' says many things.

'Welcome!' says I want to share your happiness.

What else does 'Welcome!' say?

WELCOME!_____

WELCOME!_____

WELCOME!_____

WELCOME!_____

WELCOME!_____

SAY HELLO!

Isn't it funny that we say to a new-born baby: 'Say "Hello" to your Grandma'?

We'd be very surprised if the baby actually did say 'Hello, Grandma'!

Are we silly when we do things like that?

Why do we do it?

_____

_____

_____

_____

_____

REASONS

In the box put a ✓ if you think that it is a good reason for having a baby baptized, or put a x if you think that it is not a good reason for having a baby baptized.

1. It's the thing to do. ☐

2. My family would want it. ☐

3. You have to have some kind of party
   for a new-born baby. ☐

4. I do not want my baby to go to limbo. ☐

5. I want my baby to have what I have. ☐

6. I think it's the right way to start off
   my baby's life. ☐

7. Jesus is important to me, and I want my
   baby to know Jesus. ☐

8. After buying baby clothes — it's the next
   thing to do. ☐

9. I want my baby to be part of the Church. ☐

10. I want my baby to go to a Catholic school. ☐

11. I want God to be part of my baby's life. ☐

12. It's the right thing to do. ☐

13. If a baby is not baptized it will be unlucky. ☐

Do you have a special reason of your own?

_____

_____

_____

_____

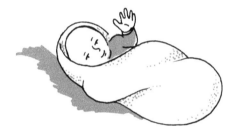

Choose the *three* most important reasons for *you.*

My three most important reasons are:

No. ____

No. ____

No. ____

RITE OF BAPTISM - I

What name have you given your child?

What do you ask of God's Church?

The parents are asked a solemn question:

'You have asked to have your child baptized. In doing so, you are accepting the responsibility of training him(her) in the practice of the faith. It will be your duty to bring him(her) up to keep God's commandments as Christ taught us, by loving God and our neighbour. Do you clearly understand what you are undertaking?'

The godparents are then asked:
'Are you ready to help the parents of this child in their duty as Christian parents?'

The priest, now calling the baby by name, says:
'The Christian community welcomes you with great joy. In its name I claim you for Christ, our Saviour, by the sign of his cross. I now trace the cross on your forehead, and invite your parents and godparents to do the same.'

9

'I have called you by name you are mine.'

The name we have chosen for our child:

We chose this name because

_____

_____

_____

_____

_____

RESPONSIBILITIES

(A) 'You are accepting the responsibility of training your child in the practice of the faith.'

What are the ways in which you will do this?

_____

_____

_____

(B) 'It will be your duty to bring your child up to keep God's commandments as Christ taught us, by loving God and our neighbour.'

How can this be done?

_____

_____

_____

_____

Do you clearly understand what you are undertaking?

_____

GODPARENTS

Choosing godparents for your baby can be a sensitive matter! It is a great honour to be asked to be a godparent. When you ask someone to take on this responsibility you are inviting that person to share in the life of your family in a very special and important way.

When you are thinking about the people you want to choose to be godparents, there are some important questions to ask, but they could all be summed up in one basic question:

WHAT IS A GODPARENT?

A godparent is someone who represents the family of the Church, which is welcoming this baby as a new member.

Because the godparents represent the family of the Church they should:
— be members of the Catholic Church and should be baptized, have been confirmed and have received Holy Communion,

— be over 16 years old, unless a different age has been established by the Diocesan Bishop,

— be practising members of the Catholic Church.

A godparent is someone who should be an example to your child of what it means to be a follower of Jesus.

Because the godparents are meant to be an example to their godchild they should:

— be able to show, by the quality of their lives, what it means to be a member of God's family,

— be people who are prepared to pray for their godchild.

A godparent is meant to be a friend and support for you in helping your baby to grow as a child of God.

Because of this the godparents should:

— be able to take an active interest in your baby's life and particularly in his(her) growth in faith.

While there must be at least one godparent who is a practising Catholic, some families may wish to invite other members of family or friends to be 'Christian witnesses' to the baptism.

RITE OF BAPTISM II

PRAYER OF EXORCISM AND THE
ANOINTING BEFORE BAPTISM WITH THE
OIL OF CATECHUMENS

The prayer of exorcism asks that God will free us from original sin.
The anointing is a sign that God will give the strength to overcome all
of life's temptations and difficulties.

PRAYER OVER THE WATER

The water that will be used to
baptize your baby will be blessed
by the priest.

RENUNCIATION OF SIN AND THE PROFESSION OF FAITH

We reject sin and proclaim the faith which we will share with the
baby.

THE BAPTISM

Your baby will become in a very special way a child of God and a
member of the Church.

THE ANOINTING AFTER
BAPTISM WITH THE OIL OF
CHRISM

This anointing is a sign that God is
calling your baby to become like
Jesus Christ and, in time, to share in
his work.

KEEP SAFE

In the next few years, there will be many times when your heart is in your mouth! In our homes there are so many everyday objects that can be hazardous for our children. We constantly have to watch them and

protect them from things that can harm them. Just as we protect their physical life, so we must protect their spiritual life. There are many things in our world that can damage and even destroy our life in God.

What do you think are the 'poisons of sin' which threaten us today?

_____

_____

_____

How can we protect our children from the damage these 'poisons' can do?

_____

_____

THIS IS OUR FAITH

I believe in God, the Father almighty,
creator of heaven and earth.

I believe in Jesus Christ, his only Son, our Lord.
He was conceived by the power of the Holy Spirit
and born of the Virgin Mary.
He suffered under Pontius Pilate,
was crucified, died and was buried.
He descended to the dead.
On the third day he rose again.
He ascended into heaven,
and is seated at the right hand of the Father.
He will come again to judge the living and the dead.

I believe in the Holy Spirit,
the holy catholic Church,
the communion of saints,
the forgiveness of sins,
the resurrection of the body,
and the life everlasting. Amen.

What does it mean to *you?*

I *believe* in God, who

_____

_____

_____

I *believe* in Jesus Christ, who

_____

_____

_____

I *believe* in the Holy Spirit, who

_____

_____

_____

CROWNED with GLORY

When I see the heavens, the work of your hands,
the moon and the stars which you arranged.
Who is _____ that you should keep
this child in mind, that you should care for my baby?
Yet you have made this one little less than a god;
with glory and honour you crown this little one
of yours!

How great
is your name
O Lord our God

LIVING MY BAPTISM

The name Christ means 'the anointed one' and when you
were baptized or *Christ*-ened (made like Christ) you were
called to share in the work of Jesus Christ, who came to us
as

a priest

— whose work is to lead people to God by
helping them to worship, teaching them to pray
and proclaiming God's word.

a prophet

— we usually think of a prophet as someone who
foretells the future, but really a prophet is someone who
proclaims to others the way God wants us to live.

a king

— in the Bible the word 'shepherd' was sometimes used
as a title for the king. Jesus is our shepherd-king, who
guides us, encourages us, feeds us, heals us and
strengthens us as we journey to God's kingdom.

As a parent, you are now called in a very special way to share in the
work of Jesus Christ. You are called to be priest, prophet and shepherd
for your baby as your baby begins the journey of life.

How can you do this?

These are some ways in which you will be able to do this in the years to come.

1. Taking my child to Mass
2. Teaching my child right from wrong
3. Teaching my child to share
4. Listening to my child
5. Telling my child stories about Jesus
6. Helping my child to say 'I'm sorry'
7. Saying night prayers with my child
8. Showing my child how to be a good friend
9. Comforting my child when things go wrong

Which of these do you think is being:

PRIEST   □   □   □

PROPHET   □   □   □

SHEPHERD-KING   □   □   □

Are there any other ways you can think of in which you can be:

PRIEST _____

PROPHET _____

SHEPHERD-KING _____

RITE OF BAPTISM III

CLOTHING WITH THE WHITE BAPTISMAL GARMENT

Your baby is wrapped in God's love. The baptismal garment reminds us that we have great dignity as children of God.

THE PRESENTATION OF THE CANDLE

Christ is our light. You are entrusted with the light of faith which has been given to your child in baptism. You must guard the light.

THE PRAYER OVER THE EARS AND MOUTH

We pray that your child may hear God's voice and respond to it. We also pray that your child will learn to proclaim God's love for all.

THE LORD'S PRAYER

Together we say the prayer of God's family — the family to which your baby now belongs.

THE BLESSINGS

You will be blessed, and we will pray that God will give you every gift you will need for the great vocation of being a parent.

WHAT'S THE POINT?

Look who's coming!
Who is it?
It's Granny!
Who is it?
It's Granny!

— What is happening in this picture?
— Do we expect the baby to say 'It's Granny'?
— Why do we say what we say?

Is there any connection between this and saying the Lord's Prayer in the Baptism ceremony?

What else does it tell us about the importance for your children of things like:

• when you put them to bed, saying 'Good night, God bless'?

• having a crucifix, holy picture or statue in your home?

• taking them to Mass even though they cannot understand what is going on?

22

A PARENT'S PRAYER

God the Father, through his Son, the
Virgin Mary's child,
has brought joy to all Christian parents,
as they see the hope of eternal life
shine on their children.
May God bless me.
I thank God for the gift of my child.
May we be one
in thanking God forever in heaven,
in Christ Jesus, our Lord.
Amen.

God is the giver of all life,
human and divine.
May God bless me,
for I will be one of the first
teachers of my child
in the ways of faith.
May I be the best of teachers,
bearing witness to the faith
by what I say and do,
in Christ Jesus, our Lord.
Amen

BAPTISM DAY

Paste a photograph of
your baby's Baptism
here.

Our baby _____

was baptized on _____

at _____

by _____

Invite those who have joined you in celebrating
your child's Baptism to sign their names in
remembrance of this great day.

www.ingramcontent.com/pod-product-compliance
Ingram Content Group UK Ltd.
Pitfield, Milton Keynes, MK11 3LW, UK
UKHW020706060325
455689UK00011B/69